© 2009 Carte Blanche Greetings Ltd ®

www.carteblanchegreetings.com

First edition for the United States published in 2010 by Barron's Educational Series, Inc.

First published in the U.K. by HarperCollins Children's Books in 2009 under the title: *Me to You—Special Mum*

The Me to You oval, Tatty Teddy signature, and bear logo are all registered trademarks of Carte Blanche Greetings Ltd.
© Carte Blanche Greetings Ltd ® P.O. Box 500, Chichester, PO20 2XZ, U.K.

All inquiries should be addressed to:
Barron's Educational Series, Inc.
250 Wireless Boulevard
Hauppauge, NY 11788
www.barronseduc.com

ISBN-13: 978-0-7641-6292-3
ISBN-10: 0-7641-6292-6

Printed in China

9 8 7 6 5 4 3 2 1

Special Mom

BARRON'S

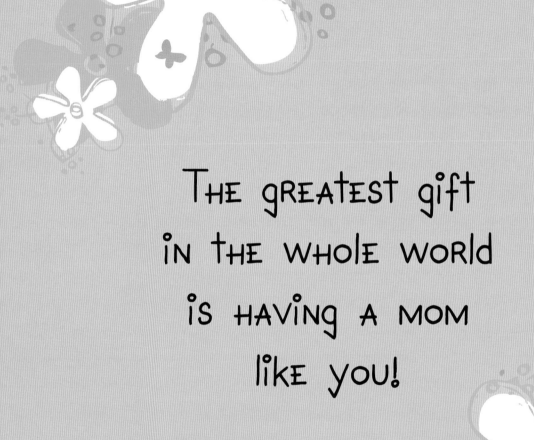

The greatest gift
in the whole world
is having a mom
like you!

When I'm with you nothing else matters.

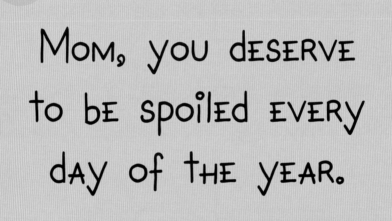

Mom, you deserve to be spoiled every day of the year.

Moms are there to dry our tears and warm our hearts.

You're the best mom
in the world and
I love you very much!

THE TIMES WE SHARE
ARE full of fun.
YOU ARE AN
AMAZING, PERFECT MOM!

Mom, you make a house into a home!

Moms are always there to lend a hand.

Mom, you are the
best friend
I could wish for.

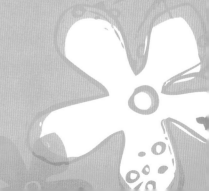

You always
lift my spirits!

It's easy to look
up to a mom like you.

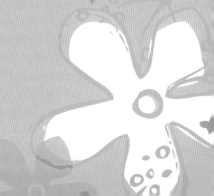

THANK YOU MOM
for all you do...
and THANK YOU MORE
for being you!